Watching the Weather

Miranda Ashwell and Andy Owen

Heinemann LIBRARY

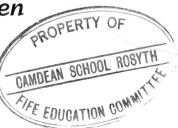

First published in Great Britain by Heinemann Library,
Halley Court, Jordan Hill, Oxford OX2 8EJ,
a division of Reed Educational and Professional Publishing Ltd.
Heinemann is a registered trademark of Reed Educational & Professional Publishing Limited.

OXFORD MELBOURNE AUCKLAND
JOHANNESBURG BLANTYRE GABORONE
IBADAN PORTSMOUTH NH (USA) CHICAGO

Designed by David Oakley
Printed and bound in Hong Kong/China

04 03 02 01 00
10 9 8 7 6 5 4 3 2 1

ISBN 0 431 03829 5
This title is also available in a hardback library edition (ISBN 0 431 03828 7)

British Library Cataloguing in Publication Data

Ashwell, Miranda
Watching the weather. - (What is weather?)
1. Weather - Juvenile literature
I. Title II. Owen, Andy
551.6

ISBN 0431038295

Acknowledgements
The Publishers would like to thank the following for permission to reproduce photographs:
Austin J Brown: p12; Bruce Coleman Limited: pp15, 23, F Labhardt p5 (upper), Pacific Stock p8; Robert Harding Picture Library: pp4 (upper), 11, 26, M Black p7, J Greenberg/MR p13, T Jones p9, G White p17; Oxford Scientific Films: NASA p20; Andy Owen: p14; Panos Pictures: Z Nelson p25; Pictor International: p16; Rex Features, London: pp28, 29; Science Photo Library: M Burnett p18, Earth Satellite Corporation p21, NASA p24, NRSC Ltd p10, D Parker p19, P Plailly/Eurelios p27; Stock Market: p5 (lower), B Harris p22, R Morsch p4 (lower).

Cover: P Menzel, Science Photo Library.

Every effort has been made to contact copyright holders of any material reproduced in this book. Any omissions will be rectified in subsequent printings if notice is given to the Publisher.

Any words appearing in the text in bold, **like this**, are explained in the Glossary.

Contents

What is weather?

Rain, sunshine, snow and wind are all types of weather. We also use the words hot and cold when we talk about weather.

We all feel the weather. On very wet days we must wear **waterproof** clothes. On warm, sunny days we like to be outside.

What will the weather be like?

We need to know what the weather will be like. It must be dry to play some sports. Rain has stopped this game of tennis.

The sea can be dangerous in windy weather. Before fishermen go out to fish, they need to know that the weather will be safe.

Weather stories

For hundreds of years people have wanted to know about the weather. There is an old story that says a red sky at night means that the next day will be dry and sunny.

Some plants can be used to test the weather. These African marigolds close their colourful petals when it is going to rain.

Weather patterns

We use photographs of Earth taken from space to find patterns in the weather. Clouds show that a **storm** is coming. No clouds show that it is hot and dry.

People use these patterns to work out what will happen to the weather.
We can see weather **forecasts** on television or in the newspapers.

How much rain?

Special aeroplanes fly into clouds to measure the amount of water inside. This helps people to know how much rain will fall.

This man is using a **rain gauge**. It is used to collect rain to tell us how much rain has fallen.

Which way is the wind blowing?

Watching the way the wind blows helps people to understand how the weather may change. This **weather vane** shows the wind is blowing from the south.

A **windsock** fills up with air. It turns with the wind and tells us which way the wind is blowing.

How fast is the wind?

The wind fills these large sails and pushes the boats along. The harder it blows, the faster the boats move.

These cups catch the wind and spin around. They measure how fast the wind is blowing. Here, the wind is blowing at 2 metres per second.

Weather balloons

This balloon carries machines that watch the weather. It will fly higher than any aeroplane. We can learn what the weather is like high above the ground.

The balloon sends messages about moving wind and rain. People use computers to look at these messages. Then they know how the weather will change.

Watching from space

Satellites in space watch the weather on Earth. They send messages and pictures back to Earth. This information teaches us more about the weather.

The Earth looks blue from space. But the colours of this satellite picture have been changed by computer. The bright colours show where it is raining.

Weather warning

Warnings are given if the weather is going to be very bad. People study the weather so they are ready when the bad weather comes.

These people have heard a danger
warning. They are using bags of sand
to stop water flooding into their houses
after heavy rain.

Danger!

This is a **satellite photo** of a
storm. Messages on the television
and radio warn people who are in
danger from the storm.

These people have been sheltering from a storm. They were safe inside this building until the wind and rain had passed.

Past weather

The weather slowly changes. These old paintings in the Sahara **Desert** show that giraffes once lived there. But now this place is too dry and dusty for giraffes.

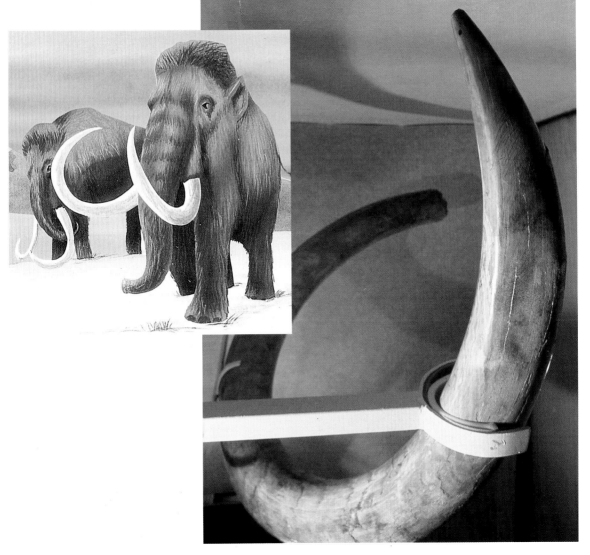

This woolly mammoth's tooth was found in England. Woolly mammoths lived long ago in cold, icy places. So we know that England was once much colder than it is now.

Changing weather

The weather is still changing. **Antarctica** is covered in thick ice. But lots of the ice is melting. Is the world getting warmer?

Things that happen on Earth can change the weather. Clouds of ash from this huge **volcano** blocked heat from the Sun. This made everywhere cooler for a few years.

It's amazing!

Strong winds called the jet stream blow high above the ground. They blow at over 200 kilometres per hour. Aeroplanes use the power of the jet stream to fly faster.

In Peru the weather **forecast** is the most popular programme on television.

Supermarkets need to know what the weather will be like. People buy more ice-cream and cold drinks when the weather is hot.

Glossary

desert   a place which is very dry, and usually very hot

forecast   information telling us what the weather is going to do

rain gauge   a tube that collects rain to show how much has fallen

satellite   a spacecraft that moves around the Earth

satellite photo   a photograph taken in space from a satellite

storm   strong wind and heavy rain

volcano   a hole in the Earth's surface through which melted rock, ash and gases escape

waterproof   something which keeps water out

weather vane   a weather vane turns in the wind to show which way it is blowing

windsock   a type of flag that shows which way the wind is blowing

Index